BETTER TOGETHER: ANIMAL GROUPS

GEESE GAGGLES

by Karen Latchana Kenney

pogo

Ideas for Parents and Teachers

Pogo Books let children practice reading informational text while introducing them to nonfiction features such as headings, labels, sidebars, maps, and diagrams, as well as a table of contents, glossary, and index.

Carefully leveled text with a strong photo match offers early fluent readers the support they need to succeed.

Before Reading

- "Walk" through the book and point out the various nonfiction features. Ask the student what purpose each feature serves.
- Look at the glossary together. Read and discuss the words.

Read the Book

- Have the child read the book independently.
- Invite him or her to list questions that arise from reading.

After Reading

- Discuss the child's questions. Talk about how he or she might find answers to those questions.
- Prompt the child to think more. Ask: Did you know groups of geese were called gaggles before you read this book? What other animal group names do you know?

Pogo Books are published by Jump!
5357 Penn Avenue South
Minneapolis, MN 55419
www.jumplibrary.com

Library of Congress Cataloging-in-Publication Data

Names: Kenney, Karen Latchana, author.
Title: Geese gaggles / by Karen Latchana Kenney.
Description: Pogo books edition.
Minneapolis, MN: Jump!, Inc., [2020]
Series: Better together: animal groups
Audience: Age 7-10. | Includes index.
Identifiers: LCCN 2018058152 (print)
LCCN 2019000014 (ebook)
ISBN 9781641288484 (ebook)
ISBN 9781641288477 (hardcover : alk. paper)
Subjects: LCSH: Geese–Behavior–Juvenile literature.
Classification: LCC QL696.A52 (ebook)
LCC QL696.A52 K46 2020 (print)
DDC 598.4/1715–dc23
LC record available at https://lccn.loc.gov/2018058152

Editor: Jenna Trnka
Designer: Jenna Casura

Photo Credits: ChungPhotoStory/Shutterstock, cover; alexmak7/Shutterstock, 1; Kasikun_Kamol/Shutterstock, 3; Feng Yu/Shutterstock, 4; july7th/iStock, 5; Chris Strickland/iStock, 6-7; Delmas Lehman/Shutterstock, 8-9; saiko3p/Shutterstock, 10-11 (background); Sunil Sharma/iStock, 10-11 (geese); SharonFoelz/iStock, 12; Marv Vandehey/Shutterstock, 13; Avalon/Photoshot License/Alamy, 14-15; Alexander Sviridov/Shutterstock, 16; John Cancalosi/Age Fotostock, 17; Geoffrey Kuchera/Shutterstock, 18-19; Jesse Seniunas/Shutterstock, 20-21; Kukota/Shutterstock, 23.

Printed in the United States of America at Corporate Graphics in North Mankato, Minnesota.

TABLE OF CONTENTS

CHAPTER 1

GAGGLES AND FLOCKS

Honk! Honk! Geese call out loudly as they take off from a pond. A group of geese on land or in water is called a **gaggle**.

In the air, a group of flying geese is a **flock**. A snow geese flock can have 1,000 birds!

Many geese fly together. In fall, they **migrate** south. They fly to warmer places for the winter. In spring, they fly back north again. They go to the same places every year.

They fly in a V shape. Why? It is easy to see each other in this **formation**. They honk to one another. They keep track of all birds in the flock.

One goose is at the point of the V. It is an older bird. It has made this flight many times. This goose leads the flock.

leader

Bar-headed geese fly higher than any other migrating bird. They even fly over mountains! Flying in groups helps geese save **energy**. It helps them fly farther. How?

Birds at the front fly lower. Wind comes off of their wings. It helps lift the birds behind. Tired birds move from the front to the back. They can flap their wings less.

TAKE A LOOK!

Wind swirls off the top of a goose's wings. It moves back. It pushes up on the wings of the geese behind.

CHAPTER 2

PROTECTION IN NUMBERS

Flying works up an appetite. The flock stops to eat grasses, seeds, and plants. Some eat fish or insects, too. This one dives for water plants!

Flocks look for places to stop. This flock finds a large, open field. It has few trees. It also has plenty of food for the geese to eat.

The many eyes in the group watch. **Predators** can attack when geese are on the ground. Coyotes or foxes might be near. If geese see predators, they honk. The gaggle quickly takes to the sky.

DID YOU KNOW?

Healthy geese will leave the flock to tend to a sick or injured member. They find it food. They protect it from predators, too.

CHAPTER 3

GEESE FAMILIES

In spring, the flock breaks apart. Why? It is time to **mate**. A male and a female pair up.

The pair stays together for life. The female makes a nest. She adds grasses and **down**. Then she lays two to eight eggs.

gosling

The father protects the nest. He chases away predators that want to eat the eggs. After around 30 days, the eggs **hatch**. **Goslings** break out of their shells.

The family stays together for about one year. Then the young birds fly off to be with other birds in the flock.

DID YOU KNOW?

Goslings learn quickly! After only 24 hours, they can already walk and swim.

The weather gets colder. It is time to migrate south again. Small families join together. They create a group. Together, the flock will make a long journey. They need each other to survive.

DID YOU KNOW?

Most wild geese live up to 12 years. Some live much longer. They can live up to 30 years!

ACTIVITIES & TOOLS

TRY THIS!

FLY LIKE GEESE

Geese flocks fly in a V shape. They switch places while they fly, too. Try to fly like geese in this activity.

What You Need:

- a few friends
- a big empty space

1. Gather a few friends together. Stand in a V shape. One person should be at the point of the V.
2. Now start running together. Try to stay in the V shape. Is it hard or easy?
3. Next, try to switch places while moving. Have the leader move to the back of the formation. At the same time, the person behind should move up. This is the new leader.
4. Did you stay in the V shape? Was it hard or easy to switch places? Try again to see if you get better with practice.

GLOSSARY

down: The layer of fine feathers underneath the tougher feathers on the outside.

energy: The ability or strength to do things without getting tired.

flock: A group of geese in the air.

formation: A pattern or shape.

gaggle: A group of geese that is not in flight.

goslings: Young geese.

hatch: To break out of an egg.

mate: To join together to produce babies.

migrate: To move to another area or climate at a particular time of year.

predators: Animals that hunt other animals for food.

INDEX

TO LEARN MORE

Finding more information is as easy as 1, 2, 3.

1. Go to www.factsurfer.com
2. Enter "geesegaggles" into the search box.
3. Choose your book to see a list of websites.

FACT SURFER